Illustrator:
Ken Tunell

Editorial Project Manager:
Charles Payne M.A., M.F.A.

Editor:
Evan D. Forbes, M.S. Ed.

Editor in Chief:
Sharon Coan, M.S. Ed.

Creative Director:
Elayne Roberts

Art Coordinator:
Cheri Macoubrie Wilson

Cover Series Design:
Tina DeLeon Macabitas

Cover Artist:
Denise Bauer

Product Manager:
Phil Garcia

Imaging:
Evan D. Forbes, M.S. Ed.
James Edward Grace

Publishers:
Rachelle Cracchiolo, M.S. Ed.
Mary Dupuy Smith, M.S. Ed.

INTERNET ACTIVITIES FOR SCIENCE

PRIMARY

Author:

Alain Chirinian

Teacher Created Materials, Inc.
6421 Industry Way
Westminster, CA 92683
www.teachercreated.com

ISBN-1-57690-409-1

©1999 Teacher Created Materials, Inc.

Made in U.S.A.

Teacher Created Materials

TABLE OF CONTENTS

Introduction 4

Our Closest Neighbor (Astronomy) 5

High Flying Snowball (Astronomy) 7

Dry, Dusty Death Valley (Life/Earth Science) 9

Cuddly Koalas (Life Science) 11

Hefty, Happy Hippo! (Life Science) 13

Famous Frog Tales (Life Science) 15

Tiger Time! (Life Science) 17

More Tigers, Please (Life Science) 19

Along Came a Spider (Life Science) 21

Swamp Mania (Life Science) 23

Desert Crystals (Earth Science) 25

At the Zoo (Life Science) 27

A Puzzling Ocean (Life Science) 29

Save the Mermaid! (Life Science) 31

Landing on Mars (Astronomy) 33

Which Animal Is It? (Life Science) 35

Get to Know the Gray Whale (Life Science) 37

In the Arctic (Life Science) 39

Birds on Ice (Life Science) 41

Touch That Tank (Life Science) 43

A Forest Wetland (Life Science) 45

All Quiet in the Wetlands (Life Science) 47

What's the Weather? (Earth Science) 49

Weather Disasters (Earth Science) 51

Just a Hiccup! (Life Science) 53

It's an Ear Thing (Life Science) 55

Morning Breath! (Life Science/Health) 57

The Yuckiest Insect (Life Science) 59

Stuck on Ice (Physical/Life Science) 61

Different States, Different Flakes (Earth Science) 63

Seek, and You Might Find It (Life Science) 65

Old Bones (Earth/Life Science) 67

Howling Wolves (Life Science) 69

Colorful Crayons (Physical Science/Technology) 71

Eat Your Fruits and Vegetables! (Life Science) 73

Make Your Own Dinosaur! (Life Science) 75

TABLE OF CONTENTS *(cont.)*

Puzzling Animals (Life Science) 77

Herd Those Sheep (Life Science) 79

Being Green (Life Science/Ecology) 81

Just the Bear Facts (Life Science) 83

Our Solar System (Earth/Space Science) 85

Solar System Matching (Earth Science) 87

Into Orbits We Go (Earth/Space Science) 89

Space Words to Know (Astronomy) 91

A Trip to the Zoo (Life Science) 93

Fins, Tails, and More (Life Science) 95

Be Good to Nature (Life Science) 97

Save Our Creatures (Life Science) 99

A World for Chipmunks (Life Science/Ecology) 101

Clean That Water! (Physical Science/Ecology) 103

Help Save a Tree! (Life Science) 105

Are You Allergic? (Life Science) 107

Zit Back and Relax (Life Science) 109

Froggy Time! (Life Science) 111

You Are Eating Right, Right? (Life Science/Health) 113

Eat or Be Eaten (Life Science) 115

Build a Custom Car (Technology/Physical Science) 117

Where Did It Go? (Life Science) 119

Going Batty! (Life Science) 121

Its a Rat Game (Life Science) 123

Space Science Matching (Astronomy) 125

Your Own Computer Fish Tank! (Life Science) 127

High Energy Fun! (Physical Science) 129

Taking Care of Tiger (Life Science) 131

Can You Guess the Animals? (Life Science) 133

A Desert Visit (Life Science) 135

Penguin Scramble (Life Science) 137

Shipwrecked! (Physical Science/Life Science) 139

It's About Trees (Life Science) 141

Making Tracks (Life Science) 143

INTRODUCTION

Many teachers have access to the Internet in a classroom setting. And many of those same teachers are asking themselves the question: Now that I have it, just what do I do with it? Will it be unique, a meaningful experience, or just something that I could have done with printed materials? Whether you have a well-equipped computer lab or just a single machine, like all teachers you want to make the best possible use of this new tool for student learning, involvement, and achievement.

This book is designed to help you take full advantage of the most important new learning opportunity ever available to our students: the Internet. In order to be competitive thinkers, workers, and productive citizens with high self-esteem, the young people whom we teach must become familiar with this latest communication tool. *Internet Activities for Science* presents a special way for students to launch themselves onto the World Wide Web, visiting virtual zoos, universities, museums, and even outer space while learning improtant science information and having fun while doing it.

Teacher pages are provided for each activity to help familiarize you with the objectives to be accomplished. In addition, tips regarding preparation for the lessons as well as suggestions on how to integrate the use of each lesson into your curriculum add a further dimension to this quick and easy format.

Internet Activities for Science assumes that you have a basic knowledge of Internet use and terminology and can move freely around the World Wide Web as needed. It is important that you upgrade your browser to the latest version available and enable its Java capabilities. Furthermore, you should take advantage of the many helper applications, or "plug-ins," available, such as *Shockwave* and *RealAudio* for the best results on some Web sites.

You may want your students to bookmark the sites they go to frequently. Bookmarking a Web site allows you to go back to a particular site without spending a large quantity of time getting there, because it is already saved in the computer's memory. To bookmark, click Favorites on your browser tool bar, then select the option that says "make this a favorite," and then okay it. Finally, be sure that you double-check that the Web site or links from a Web site are stlll active before you assign an acitivty. With the fast pace of change on the Internet, some sites may have moved or been depowered in the interim since this book was written.

Teacher Created Materials attempts to offset this ongoing problem by posting changes of URL's on our Web site. Check our home page at www.teachercreated.com for updates on this book.

One method of cheating the fickle nature of the Web is to use a Web "whacking" program, such as *Web Buddy*, produced by DataViz. *Web Buddy* will allow you to "whack" or download a single Web page or even an entire Web site, including the links and graphics. It stores the Web pages on your hard drive where they can be accessed with your browser at a later date—even if the page or site has disappeared! Students can enjoy the Web-based activities without the associated wait times during peak Internet hours, or the dreaded "Not Found" error. Teacher Created Materials publishes *Web Buddy*, a book filled with classroom projects and tips on using the *Web Buddy* software which is included on a CD-ROM. It is available for $39.95 by calling (800) 662-4321.

OUR CLOSEST NEIGHBOR

Content Area(s):

- astronomy

Objectives:

Students will . . .

- read facts about the moon.
- determine how the moon relates to the earth.

Materials Required:

- computer with Internet access
- pencil or pen

Web Site(s):

- http://www.frontiernet.net/~kidpower/moon.html

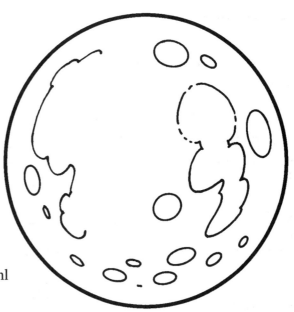

Time:

approximately 25–35 minutes

Teaching the Lesson:

- Preview this lesson with a discussion of the Apollo space program.
- This activity is for good readers or pairs of students.
- You may want to discuss legends of the moon, such as man in the moon, etc., as a follow-up activity.

OUR CLOSEST NEIGHBOR *(cont.)*

Name:_____

Date:_____

Go to http://www.frontiernet.net/~kidpower/moon.html and read the information about the moon on this Internet page. Answer the questions below.

1. Are there objects in space besides the moon that have been visited by people?

   _____

   _____

2. How long does it take for the moon to make one orbit around the earth?

   _____

   _____

3. What caused the craters on the moon?

   _____

   _____

4. Why can the moon be seen without a telescope?

   _____

   _____

5. Is the moon really made of green cheese? Explain your answer.

   _____

   _____

HIGH FLYING SNOWBALL

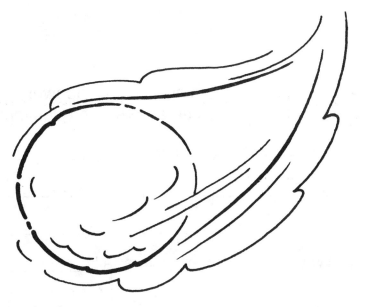

Content Area(s):

- astronomy

Objectives:

Students will . . .

- read about comets.
- determine and record basic facts about comets.

Materials Required:

- computer with Internet access
- pencil or pen

Web Site(s):

- http://www.frontiernet.net/~kidpower/comet.html

Time:

approximately 25–35 minutes

Teaching the Lesson:

- Preview this activity with a discussion of what kinds of things are found moving in outer space.
- This activity is for good readers or pairs of students.
- Have students predict or learn details about the next comet due in their lifetime. They can calculate how old they will be when it arrives.

HIGH FLYING SNOWBALL *(cont.)*

Name:_____

Date:_____

Go to http://www.frontiernet.net/~kidpower/comet.html and read about comets on this Web page. Then answer the questions below.

1. What are comets made of? _____

_____

_____

2. Why does a comet have a tail? _____

_____

_____

3. How could you have a comet named after you? _____

_____

_____

4. Name two famous comets. _____

_____

_____

5. If you saw a comet streaking through the sky, would you be afraid? Explain why or why not. _____

_____

_____

_____

_____

DRY, DUSTY DEATH VALLEY

Content Area(s):

- life science
- earth science

Objectives:

Students will . . .

- read about the desert biome.
- determine how the desert biome is different from other biomes.
- draw a picture of a desert.

Materials Required:

- computer with Internet access
- pencil or pen
- drawing materials

Web Site(s):

- http://www.exploratorium.edu/learning_studio/news/january98.html

Time:

approximately 25–35 minutes

Teaching the Lesson:

- A discussion of where deserts are located and their importance to the environment is a good preview activity.
- This activity is for good readers or pairs of students.
- You should discuss the extreme temperatures at Death Valley by providing students with concrete examples (or brainstorm with them) of what it feels like at 80, 90, 100 degrees, etc.

DRY, DUSTY DEATH VALLEY *(cont.)*

Name:_____

Date:_____

Go to http://www.exploratorium.edu/learning_studio/news/january98.html and read about the most famous desert in the United States, Death Valley. Then answer the questions below.

1. How do you suppose Death Valley got its name? _____

   _____

2. What was the hottest temperature ever at Death Valley? _____

3. Name three kinds of animals that can live in a desert like Death Valley. ____

   _____

   _____

4. Do you think it ever gets cold in Death Valley? Explain your answer. _____

   _____

   _____

   _____

5. Draw a picture below of an animal or plant that you might expect to find in Death Valley.

CUDDLY KOALAS

Content Area(s):

- life science

Objectives:

Students will . . .

- listen to the sounds of a koala.
- compare the koala with familiar animals.
- take an online koala quiz.

Materials Required:

- computer with Internet access
- pencil or pen

Web Site(s):

- http://www.zooregon.org/Koalas/koalas_are_coming.htm
- http://www.bconnex.net/~kidworld/koa.htm

Time:

approximately 25–35 minutes

Teaching the Lesson:

- A discussion of Australia, endangered animals, and even marsupials is an excellent introduction to this topic.
- This activity is for good readers or pairs of students.
- Go over the things students learned about koalas as a closure activity.

CUDDLY KOALAS *(cont.)*

Name:_____

Date:_____

Go to http://www.zooregon.org/Koalas/koalas_are_coming.htm

Look at the picture of the koala on this Web page. Then listen to it by clicking on the link shown.

1. What does the koala sound like to you? _____

   _____

2. Look at the picture of the koala. Does it look like an animal that spends more time in a tree or on the ground?_____

   _____

Go to http://www.bconnex.net/~kidworld/koa.htm

Take the koala quiz. You may check your answers on the Web page.

Write below three things you learned about koalas from this quiz.

I learned that:

a. _____

   _____

   _____

b. _____

   _____

   _____

c. _____

   _____

   _____

12   © *Teacher Created Materials, Inc.*

HEFTY, HAPPY HIPPO!

Content Area(s):

- life science

Objectives:

Students will . . .

- read about hippos.
- discuss and record facts about hippos.

Materials Required:

- computer with Internet access
- pencil or pen

Web Site(s):

- http://www.zooregon.org/cards/hippo.htm

Time:

approximately 25–35 minutes

Teaching the Lesson:

- This activity is a good part of an African animal unit. You may also discuss how these animals differ from seals and sea lions which also spend much of their lives in the water.
- This activity is for good readers or pairs of students.
- Show a video of hippos as a follow-up or introductory activity.

HEFTY, HAPPY HIPPO! *(cont.)*

Name:_____

Date:_____

Go to http://www.zooregon.org/cards/hippo.htm

Look at the picture of the hippopotamus on this Web page. Then find the answers to the questions below.

1. How much can a hippo weigh? _____

_____

2. Why does the hippo spend so much time in the water? _____

_____

_____

3. How old is an old hippo? _____

_____

4. What are hippos fed in the zoo? _____

_____

_____

5. Where (besides the zoo) might you expect to find a hippo? _____

_____

_____

FAMOUS FROG TALES

Content Area(s):

- life science

Objectives:

Students will . . .

- interpret a picture of a frog's unusual activities.
- record information about an extinct frog.

Materials Required:

- computer with Internet access
- pencil or pen

Web Site(s):

- http://www.teleport.com/~dstroy/weird/strange/brooding.html

Time:

approximately 25–35 minutes

Teaching the Lesson:

- You should introduce this topic along with a unit on amphibians.
- This activity is for good readers or pairs of students.
- Emphasize that students should consider the pictures before reading about them on the Web site.
- Explain the concept of extinction. Give examples of extinct animals they are familiar with.

FAMOUS FROG TALES *(cont.)*

Name:_____

Date:_____

Go to http://www.teleport.com/~dstroy/weird/strange/brooding.html

Look carefully at the picture of the two frogs. Write down what you see on this page without reading about it.

I think this is a picture of

Now read the information about what you are really seeing in this picture.

1. Where does the baby frog live?_____

   _____

2. Where was this frog once found? _____

   _____

3. This frog is now thought to be extinct. What does that mean?_____

   _____

   _____

   _____

TIGER TIME!

Content Area(s):

- life science

Objectives:

Students will . . .

- read about tigers.
- compare tigers from different areas in the world.
- describe tiger extinctions.

Materials Required:

- computer with Internet access
- pencil or pen

Web Site(s):

- http://www.5tigers.org/coolfac.htm

Time:

approximately 25–35 minutes

Teaching the Lesson:

- An introduction to tiger legends, tiger poems, and tiger stories would engage students in this topic.
- This activity is for good readers or pairs of students.
- Discuss the causes of extinction, including human and natural causes.

TIGER TIME! *(cont.)*

Name:_____

Date:_____

Go to http://www.5tigers.org/coolfac.htm and read the fun facts about tigers on this Web page. Then find the answers to the questions below.

1. How many different kinds of tigers are there in the world today? _____
   _____

2. Name all the kinds of tigers found in the world._____
   _____
   _____
   _____

3. How many tigers are left in the wild?_____
   _____

4. Three kinds of tigers have become extinct in the past 70 years. Name these tigers.

   _____
   _____
   _____

5. Click on the word *extinct*. What does it mean?_____
   _____
   _____
   _____
   _____

MORE TIGERS, PLEASE

Content Area(s):

- life science

Objectives:

Students will . . .

- answer questions on tiger facts.
- draw a picture of a tiger in its environment.

Materials Required:

- computer with Internet access
- pencil or pen
- drawing materials

Web Site(s):

- http://www.5tigers.org/talkback/talk.htm

Time:

approximately 25–35 minutes

Teaching the Lesson:

- Be sure students are able to click on links and return to the original Web page to do this activity.
- This activity is for good readers or pairs of students.
- Have students read their picture captions aloud to the class when they are finished.

MORE TIGERS, PLEASE *(cont.)*

Name:_____

Date:_____

Go to http://www.5tigers.org/talkback/talk.htm and read the Web page. Click on the links to find the answers to the questions below about tigers.

1. Why do tigers have stripes?_____

   _____

2. How fast can tigers run? _____

   _____

3. Are tigers people eaters?_____

   _____

On the rest of this page, draw a picture of a tiger in the grass. Then explain what is happening in your picture.

ALONG CAME A SPIDER

Content Area(s):

- life science

Objectives:

Students will . . .

- read poems and stories depicting spiders.
- interpret a Native American spider legend.

Materials Required:

- computer with Internet access
- pencil or pen

Web Site(s):

- http://dns.ufsia.ac.be/Arachnology/Pages/Kids.html
- http://dns.ufsia.ac.be/Arachnology/Pages/A_stories.html#story1

Time:

approximately 25–35 minutes

Teaching the Lesson:

- Brainstorm with students about spiders in stories, songs, and poems to begin this activity.
- This activity is for good readers or pairs of students.
- Have students write a poem or story of their own about a spider as a follow-up activity.

ALONG CAME A SPIDER *(cont.)*

Name:_____

Date:_____

Go to http://dns.ufsia.ac.be/Arachnology/Pages/Kids.html and read the Mother Goose nursery rhyme on this page. Answer the questions below.

1. Why was Miss Muffet afraid? _____

   _____

   _____

   _____

2. Do you think that most spiders are really dangerous to people? _____

   _____

   _____

   _____

Go to http://dns.ufsia.ac.be/Arachnology/Pages/A_stories.html#story1

Read the Native American story called "The Fire and the Spider." Then answer the questions below.

3. Whose was the tiny voice in the story? _____

   _____

   _____

4. What is the little "pot" on the back of the water spider called today? _____

   _____

   _____

SWAMP MANIA

Content Area(s):

- life science

Objectives:

Students will . . .

- identify native plants and animals in swamps.
- distinguish between day-and night-active animals.

Materials Required:

- computer with Internet access
- pencil or pen

Web Site(s):

- http://www.auduboninstitute.org/html/interswampmain.html

Time:

approximately 25–35 minutes

Teaching the Lesson:

- Explain the value of a "swamp" area to students. They should be made aware before doing this activity that these are not wasteland areas to be filled with dirt.
- This activity is for good readers or pairs of students.
- Discuss the states where swamps are found and some of the human cultures (i.e., Cajuns) and the traditions associated with them.

SWAMP MANIA *(cont.)*

Name:_____

Date:_____

Go to http://www.auduboninstitute.org/html/interswampmain.html

After the Web page loads, click continue and find the answers to the questions below.

1. What is the name of the fish with the long nose? _____

_____

2. What is special about the person in the rowboat?_____

_____

_____

3. Is the snake you see a dangerous one? _____

_____

Switch to nighttime by clicking the day/night button.

4. What kind of bird is fishing now?_____

_____

5. What is the name of the owl you can see and hear at night in the swamp?

_____

_____

24

DESERT CRYSTALS

Content Area(s):

- earth science

Objectives:

Students will . . .

- identify crystals by shape and color.
- read about caves.

Materials Required:

- computer with Internet access
- pencil or pen

Web Site(s):

- http://www.desert.net/museum/cave/CAVE1.HTML

Time:

approximately 25–35 minutes

Teaching the Lesson:

- You should bring in examples of crystals to class, such as stone, glass, or costume jewelry.
- This activity is for good readers or pairs of students.
- Make some crystals in class, using salt and water (directions found in any beginning science book).

DESERT CRYSTALS *(cont.)*

Name:_____

Date:_____

Go to http://www.desert.net/museum/cave/CAVE1.HTML

Click the button to find the names of five crystals found in the desert caves. Write down the name of each crystal you see. Then write a description that includes the colors and shapes of the crystals.

Crystal Name	**Description**
1._____	_____ _____
2._____	_____ _____
3._____	_____ _____
4._____	_____ _____
5._____	_____ _____

AT THE ZOO

Content Area(s):

- life science

Objectives:

Students will . . .

- choose animals from a "virtual zoo."
- write a summary of each animal's appearance and habits.

Materials Required:

- computer with Internet access
- pencil or pen

Web Site(s):

- http://www.birminghamzoo.com/animals

Time:

approximately 25–35 minutes

Teaching the Lesson:

- Be sure students understand what to write after they choose each animal.
- This activity is for good readers or pairs of students.
- Have students compare their favorite animals with other students. They should see if they described common animals the same way or differently. Then they can add more things to their own descriptions.

AT THE ZOO *(cont.)*

Name:_____

Date:_____

Go to http://www.birminghamzoo.com/animals

Pick three animals listed on this Web page. Click on the links you have chosen.
Then write three sentences about each animal.

The first animal I chose is called a _____

_____

_____

_____

_____.

The second animal I chose is called a _____

_____

_____

_____

The third animal I chose is called a _____

_____

_____

_____

_____

A PUZZLING OCEAN

Content Area(s):

- life science

Objectives:

Students will . . .

- solve ocean-related puzzles.
- record ocean information they learn.

Materials Required:

- computer with Internet access
- pencil or pen

Web Site(s):

- http://www.seasky.org/sea4b.html

Time:

approximately 25–35 minutes

Teaching the Lesson:

- Review with students exactly how to maneuver puzzle pieces when solving this type of puzzle.
- This activity is for good readers or pairs of students.
- They must write down a description of what happens once they solve the puzzle. Be sure they understand what you are looking for (do an example for them).

A PUZZLING OCEAN *(cont.)*

Name:_____

Date:_____

Go to http://www.seasky.org/sea4b.html

On this Web page you will see strange creatures from the sea come to life if you can solve the puzzles. Click on a puzzle piece to move it to the blank space. Solve three puzzles. After you solve a puzzle, write down what you see.

Puzzle One Description: _____

_____

_____

_____

_____

Puzzle Two Description:_____

_____

_____

_____

_____

Puzzle Three Description: _____

_____

_____

_____

_____

SAVE THE MERMAID!

Content Area(s):

- life science

Objectives:

Students will . . .

- discuss mermaid legends.
- express how they would feel if they encountered a mermaid.
- explain how mermaids and real animals compare.

Materials Required:

- computer with Internet access
- pencil or pen

Web Site(s):

- http://www.seasky.org/sea4d.html

Time:

approximately 25–35 minutes

Teaching the Lesson:

- Take some time to go over the legend of the mermaid before doing this activity.
- This activity is for good readers or pairs of students.
- You may want to expand on the answers to the last question as a class discussion.

SAVE THE MERMAID! *(cont.)*

Name:_____

Date:_____

Go to http://www.seasky.org/sea4d.html

On this Web page, you will play a game to try to save the mermaid from the sharks. After you finish the game, answer the questions below.

1. Is a mermaid real or imaginary? How do you know?_____

   _____

   _____

   _____

2. In what ways does a mermaid look like a fish?_____

   _____

   _____

   _____

3. In what ways does a mermaid look like a person? _____

   _____

   _____

   _____

4. Years ago, sailors on the ocean would imagine that they saw a mermaid. What would you do if you saw a mermaid?_____

   _____

   _____

   _____

LANDING ON MARS

Content Area(s):

- astronomy

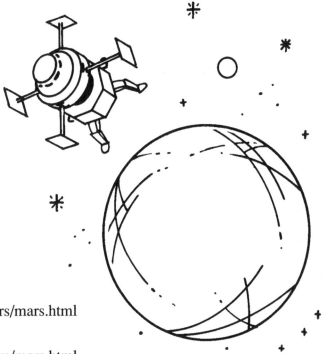

Objectives:

Students will . . .

- read facts about Mars.
- research the Internet about Mars.
- attempt to land a virtual spacecraft on Mars.

Materials Required:

- computer with Internet access
- pencil or pen

Web Site(s):

- http://observe.ivv.nasa.gov/nasa/fun/mars/mars.html
- http://www.yahooligans.com
- http://observe.ivv.nasa.gov/nasa/fun/mars/mars.html

Time:

approximately 25–35 minutes

Teaching the Lesson:

- Go over the basics of the solar system before doing this activity.
- This activity is for advanced students or pairs of students.
- The game at the end can extend the time of this activity to one hour.

LANDING ON MARS *(cont.)*

Name:_____

Date:_____

Go to http://observe.ivv.nasa.gov/nasa/fun/mars/mars.html

Landing on the planet Mars has been a dream for scientists and kids for many years. NASA has landed robots on Mars, but now is your chance to land on Mars in your own spaceship. Before you can play the game, you must answer the questions below.

Go to http://www.yahooligans.com

Type in the word "Mars" and then write three things about this planet below.

1. _____

_____

2. _____

_____

3. _____

_____

Now go back and play the Mars Lander game at this link:
http://observe.ivv.nasa.gov/nasa/fun/mars/mars.html

See if you can land the spaceship on Mars.

WHICH ANIMAL IS IT?

Content Area(s):

- life science

Objectives:

Students will . . .

- observe as the computer guesses the animals they think of.
- record the questions asked by the computer as it guesses.

Materials Required:

- computer with Internet access
- pencil or pen

Web Site(s):

- http://www.bushnet.qld.edu.au/animal

Time:

approximately 25–35 minutes

Teaching the Lesson:

- This Web site does contain several spelling errors. You can give students extra points for finding the mistakes.
- This activity is for good readers or pairs of students.
- Students must record the information at each step for this to be a successful activity.

WHICH ANIMAL IS IT? *(cont.)*

Name:_____

Date:_____

Everyone has a favorite animal. Do you think the computer can guess which one is your favorite?

Go to http://www.bushnet.qld.edu.au/animal

Follow the directions on the Web page. Write down the answer to each question in a sentence that the computer asks. Let's begin.

Question: **Answer:**

1. _____

2. _____

3. _____

4. _____

5. _____

6. _____

7. _____

8. _____

9. _____

10. _____

Did the computer guess your animal correctly? _____

What is the name of your favorite animal? _____

Write a sentence about why this animal is your favorite. _____

_____

GET TO KNOW THE GRAY WHALE

Content Area(s):

- life science

Objectives:

Students will . . .

- read about gray whales.
- describe habits of gray whales.

Materials Required:

- computer with Internet access
- pencil or pen

Web Site(s):

- http://www.whaletimes.org/whagray.htm

Time:

approximately 25–35 minutes

Teaching the Lesson:

- Explain to students the feeding habits of baleen whales and those that eat larger prey before going into detail about gray whales.
- This activity is for good readers or pairs of students.
- Students should discuss why whales are considered to be mammals and not fish, along with what humans and whales have in common.

GET TO KNOW THE GRAY WHALE *(cont.)*

Name:_____

Date:_____

Go to http://www.whaletimes.org/whagray.htm and read about gray whales on this Web page. Then find the answers to the questions below.

1. How much can a female gray whale weigh? _____

   _____

2. Where might you find a gray whale? _____

   _____

3. What is a baby gray whale called? _____

   _____

4. Do gray whales have teeth? _____

   _____

5. What do gray whales eat? _____

   _____

   _____

6. Would you be afraid of a gray whale if you saw one? Why or why not?

   _____

   _____

   _____

   _____

IN THE ARCTIC

Content Area(s):

- life science

Objectives:

Students will . . .
- research the arctic biome.
- describe characteristics of the arctic biome.

Materials Required:

- computer with Internet access
- pencil or pen

Web Site(s):

- http://dlt.gsfc.nasa.gov/Ask/lessons/regions/arctic/page1.html

Time:

approximately 25–35 minutes

Teaching the Lesson:

- Discuss with students where the Poles are located, along with the reasons that there are so few people living in these areas.
- This activity is for good readers or pairs of students.
- Study human habits and cultures from these cold regions and compare them to some animal habits in the same areas. How are they dependent on each other?

IN THE ARCTIC *(cont.)*

Name:_____

Date:_____

Go to http://dlt.gsfc.nasa.gov/Ask/lessons/regions/arctic/page1.html

On this Web page you will see a map. There are questions for you to answer. When you think you know the answer to a question, write it down below. Then press the "continue" button. When you are finished, you will have a paper showing what you learned about the Arctic.

1. Is the Arctic "on top" or on the "bottom" of the world? or both top and bottom?_____

   _____

2. If you don't live in the Arctic, which region do you live in? tropics or temperate?_____

   _____

3. What are the two seasons in the Arctic? _____

   _____

4. Name five animals that you would find in the Arctic._____

   _____

   _____

   _____

BIRDS ON ICE

Content Area(s):

- life science

Objectives:

Students will . . .

- read about the habits of penguins.
- summarize what they learned about penguins.
- draw a picture of penguins.

Materials Required:

- computer with Internet access
- pencil or pen
- drawing materials

Web Site(s):

- http://www.lpzoo.com/tour/seabird.html
- http://www.sunnyweb.com/Iceblox.htm

Time:

approximately 25–35 minutes

Teaching the Lesson:

- Discuss how penguins resemble animals other than birds.
- This activity is for good readers or pairs of students.
- The penguin game they will play can be used as a reward for a good performance on this activity.

BIRDS ON ICE *(cont.)*

Name:_____

Date:_____

Penguins live in some of the coldest places on earth, such as the North Pole. They eat fish and shrimp and are excellent swimmers. Many people think penguins look like they are wearing tuxedos. Let's find out more about this special bird that spends a lot of time on the ice.

Go to http://www.lpzoo.com/tour/seabird.html

Write down three things that you learned about penguins on this Web page.

1. _____

_____

2. _____

_____

3. _____

_____

Draw a picture below of the penguin you learned about.

When you finish, **Go to** http://www.sunnyweb.com/Iceblox.htm

Play the penguin game for fun.

TOUCH THAT TANK

Content Area(s):

- life science

Objectives:

Students will . . .

- identify ocean creatures in a "touch tank."
- describe the movements and habits of these creatures.

Materials Required:

- computer with Internet access
- pencil or pen

Web Site(s):

- http://oberon.educ.sfu.ca/splash/tank.htm

Time:

approximately 25–35 minutes

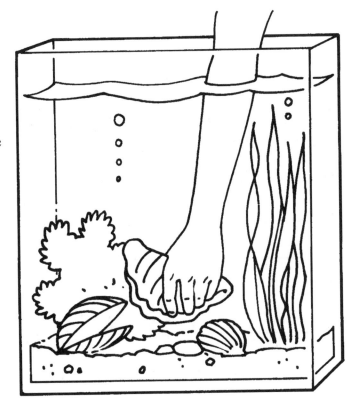

Teaching the Lesson:

- When students write down a fact, it should be one they observe from the tank experience, not from prior knowledge. This is a good way to practice observation skills.
- This activity is for good readers or pairs of students.
- You may want to allow students to earn extra credit by reporting on more than five creatures from the tank.

TOUCH THAT TANK *(cont.)*

Name:_____

Date:_____

Go to http://oberon.educ.sfu.ca/splash/tank.htm

"Touch" five of the creatures in the fish tank on this Web page. Write down the names of each one. Then write down one thing about each creature.

Creatures I "touched":

1. _____

_____

2. _____

_____

3. _____

_____

4. _____

_____

5. _____

_____

If you would like to see the creatures in the tank "move," click on the link that says "animated." Then describe below what you see.

_____

_____

_____

_____

_____

A FOREST WETLAND

Content Area(s):

- life science

Objectives:

Students will . . .

- identify traits of a forest wetland environment.
- compose riddles about animals.

Materials Required:

- computer with Internet access
- pencil or pen

Web Site(s):

- http://athena.wednet.edu/curric/land/wetland/index.html

Time:

approximately 25–35 minutes

Teaching the Lesson:

- Spend some time explaining to students what makes a wetland different from other habitats.
- This activity is for good readers or pairs of students.
- Teach students how to write a riddle about something they know before doing that portion of the activity.
- As an extension, "publish" a compilation of several riddles by each student in a book to be given to them at the end of the unit.

A FOREST WETLAND *(cont.)*

Name:_____

Date:_____

Go to http://athena.wednet.edu/curric/land/wetland/index.html

Look at the picture of the forested wetland. Name five animals that live in this kind of wetland.

1. _____

2. _____

3. _____

4. _____

5. _____

Now write a riddle for your friend. Your riddle should be about one of the animals on your list above. Look at the example of a riddle to see what yours can be like.

Question:
What flies, quacks, and lives in the forested wetlands?

Answer:
the wood duck

Now write your own riddle and try it on your friends. _____

_____

_____

_____

46

ALL QUIET IN THE WETLANDS

Content Area(s):

- life science

Objectives:

Students will . . .

- learn about the inhabitants of wetlands.
- learn about the qualities of wetlands water.

Materials Required:

- computer with Internet access
- pencil or pen
- drawing materials

Web Site(s):

- http://athena.wednet.edu/curric/land/wetland/aquatic.html

Time:

approximately 25–35 minutes

Teaching the Lesson:

- Discuss some of the more well-known wetlands areas with students, such as the Florida Everglades, to acquaint them with this biome.
- This activity is for good readers or pairs of students.
- Make available to students material besides this Web page as a reference for the drawing activity if you wish to see some originality in the drawings.

ALL QUIET IN THE WETLANDS *(cont.)*

Name:_____

Date:_____

Go to http://athena.wednet.edu/curric/land/wetland/aquatic.html and read about the aquatic wetlands. Answer the questions below.

1. What kinds of plants might you find growing in the water of an aquatic wetland? _____

   _____

   _____

2. How deep is the water in an aquatic wetland? _____

   _____

3. How do fish use aquatic wetlands? _____

   _____

   _____

4. Draw a picture of an aquatic wetland below. Include plants and animals in your picture.

WHAT'S THE WEATHER?

Content Area(s):

- earth science

Objectives:

Students will . . .

- record daily weather data.
- create a weather chart with icons for each type of weather.

Materials Required:

- computer with Internet access
- pencil or pen
- ruler/straight edge

Web Site(s):

- http://athena.wednet.edu/curric/weather/weather.html

Time:

approximately 25–35 minutes

Teaching the Lesson:

- This activity is a good culminating or introductory activity for the study of weather and weather patterns.
- Use old newspapers to have students chart more data from before the time they observe their own weather.
- As an extension, have students compare their chart to one they create using international weather data in newspapers.

WHAT'S THE WEATHER? *(cont.)*

Name:_____

Date:_____

Go to http://athena.wednet.edu/curric/weather/weather.html

Follow the directions on the Web page. Draw your chart below. Record the weather each day for a week by drawing a picture of the pertinent weather symbol. Then answer the questions.

Weather Chart

WEATHER DISASTERS

Content Area(s):

- earth science

Objectives:

Students will . . .

- research how to prepare for weather disasters.
- compare preparation for weather disasters in the home and car.

Materials Required:

- computer with Internet access
- pencil or pen

Web Site(s):

- http://weathereye.kgan.com/cadet/disaster/prephomekit.html

Time:

approximately 25–35 minutes

Teaching the Lesson:

- Discuss with students the nature of severe weather and have them tell stories of any incidents they have experienced with extreme weather conditions.
- This activity is for good readers or pairs of students.
- Survey students to see how many of their own recommendations for severe weather preparedness their parents follow.

WEATHER DISASTERS *(cont.)*

Name:_____

Date:_____

Pretend it is winter and a huge snowstorm comes to your house, almost burying it in piles of the white stuff. Will you and your family be ready?

Go to http://weathereye.kgan.com/cadet/disaster/prephomekit.html

This Web page lists what you should have at home to be prepared for a snowstorm. Read the list and answer the questions below.

1. List five things you should have at home to get ready for a snowstorm.

   _____

   _____

   _____

2. Write down what you think these five things might be used for in a snowstorm. _____

   _____

   _____

3. On this Web page, there is a list of things that should be in your car in case you get stuck in a snowstorm. Name four of those things below.

   _____

   _____

   _____

4. What are each of those four things in your car going to be used for?

   _____

   _____

   _____

52   © *Teacher Created Materials, Inc.*

IT'S AN EAR THING

Content Area(s):

- life science

Objectives:

Students will . . .

- determine the origin of earwax.
- record information about proper ear care.

Materials Required:

- computer with Internet access
- pencil or pen

Web Site(s):

- http://www.yucky.com/body/index.ssf?/yuckystuff/earwax/jsindex.html

Time:

approximately 25–35 minutes

Teaching the Lesson:

- This is a good introductory lesson on the human body and its various functions. All students can relate to this topic and become engaged in the activity.
- This activity is for good readers or pairs of students.
- Have students demonstrate proper use of a cotton swab in class, using a model ear.

IT'S AN EAR THING *(cont.)*

Name:_____

Date:_____

Have you ever wondered what that "wax" is that comes out of your ears? Do your ears really need a wax? Let's find out the answers about earwax.

Go to http://www.yucky.com/body/index.ssf?/yuckystuff/earwax/jsindex.html

Click on all the questions in the middle of the Web page. Then answer the questions below.

1. What is earwax? _____

_____

2. Where does earwax come from?_____

_____

3. Since you shouldn't clean your ears, what happens to the old wax? _____

_____

4. What is earwax used for by your ears? _____

_____

5. Write down three things that might happen if you try to clean your ears.

_____

_____

_____

_____

MORNING BREATH!

Content Area(s):

- life science
- health

Objectives:

Students will . . .

- determine the origins of bad breath.
- record definitions of bad-breath terms.
- practice good oral hygiene.

Materials Required:

- computer with Internet access
- pencil or pen

Web Site(s):

- http://www.yucky.com/body/index.ssf?/yuckystuff/breath/jsindex.html

Time:

approximately 25–35 minutes

Teaching the Lesson:

- This is another topic that all students can relate to. It can pose a management problem unless you are careful not to allow them to call each other names in relation to any particular student's hygiene.
- This activity is for good readers or pairs of students.
- Use this topic as an introduction to the topic of microorganisms (germs) that inhabit our environment and can contaminate our food or cause us to become sick.

MORNING BREATH! *(cont.)*

Name:_____

Date:_____

Why does your mouth smell so bad when you wake up in the morning? or in the afternoon after you eat lunch? Is there anything you can do about it? Let's find out.

Go to http://www.yucky.com/body/index.ssf?/yuckystuff/breath/jsindex.html

Click on the questions in the middle of the Web page. Then answer the questions below.

1. Do you think that brushing your teeth makes your breath smell better?

   _____

2. Do you think eating certain foods can make your breath smell worse? Name two of these foods. _____

   _____

3. Do you think that eating certain foods can make your breath smell better? Name two of these foods. _____

   _____

4. What is mouth rot?_____

   _____

5. There are three bad-breath words on this Web page. Write them down below._____

   _____

   _____

6. What is a kind way to tell someone that person has bad-breath? Remember that you do not want to hurt his/her feelings._____

   _____

STUCK ON ICE

Content Area(s):

- physical science
- life science

Objectives:

Students will . . .

- determine the characteristics of ice.
- compose a story related to life on an ice floe.

Materials Required:

- computer with Internet access
- pencil or pen
- drawing materials

Web Site(s):

- http://miavx1.muohio.edu/~dragonfly/snow/icefloat.htmlx

Time:

approximately 25–35 minutes

Teaching the Lesson:

- Discuss the arctic ecosystem with students prior to this activity. Explain the importance of ocean life to the creatures on land as a food source.
- The use of a story to personalize the topic allows students some freedom to construct their own meanings out of the information you provide and they get from this Web site.
- This activity is for good readers or pairs of students.
- Take the time to discuss the nature of ice itself prior to this activity—including the uses of ice and why it floats (explained in the student work sheet).

STUCK ON ICE *(cont.)*

Name:_____

Date:_____

Go to http://miavx1.muohio.edu/~dragonfly/snow/icefloat.htmlx

Look at the picture of the person stuck on an ice island. Isn't he glad that ice floats?

When you put ice in a cup of water, it stays on top. That is because ice is really just frozen water. And when water freezes, it takes up more space. When it takes up more space, it becomes less dense and floats.

Suppose you were stuck on an ice island like the person on this Web page. Write a story below about how you would live there. What would you eat? What would you drink? How would you keep busy? Then draw a picture of yourself when you are rescued from the island of ice.

_____

_____

_____

_____

_____

_____

62

DIFFERENT STATES, DIFFERENT FLAKES

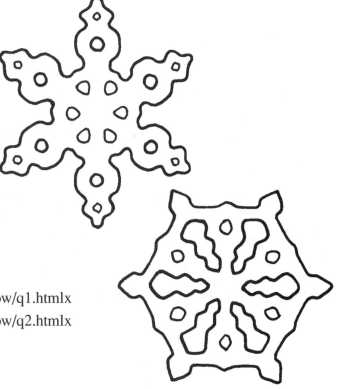

Content Area(s):

- earth science

Objectives:

Students will . . .

- determine the effect of climate on snow types.
- design a snowflake online.

Materials Required:

- computer with Internet access
- pencil or pen

Web Site(s):

- http://miavx1.muohio.edu/~dragonfly/snow/q1.htmlx
- http://miavx1.muohio.edu/~dragonfly/snow/q2.htmlx

Time:

approximately 25–35 minutes

Teaching the Lesson:

- Preview some of the vocabulary in this activity with students, particularly the shapes they need to recognize in the snowflakes.
- This activity is for advanced students or pairs of students.
- Students should have some basic knowledge of United States geography.

DIFFERENT STATES, DIFFERENT FLAKES *(cont.)*

Name:_____

Date:_____

Have you ever seen snow up close? You know that snow is made from snowflakes. But did you know that different places have different kinds of snowflakes? There are three kinds of snowflakes: plate, stellar crystal, and stud snowflakes. Your job is to see what kinds of snowflakes are found in three different states.

Go to http://miavx1.muohio.edu/~dragonfly/snow/q1.htmlx

Choose the size, temperature, and shape of snowflake you would like to see. Then click "submit."

1. Where is this kind of snowflake usually found?_____

_____

2. Draw a picture of this snowflakes below.

Go to http://miavx1.muohio.edu/~dragonfly/snow/q2.htmlx

See if you can find the kind of snowflake in the state of Ohio. Click on the size, temperature, and shape you would like to see. Then click on "submit."

3. Where is this kind of snowflake usually found?_____

_____

4. Draw a picture of this snowflake below.

SEEK, AND YOU MIGHT FIND IT

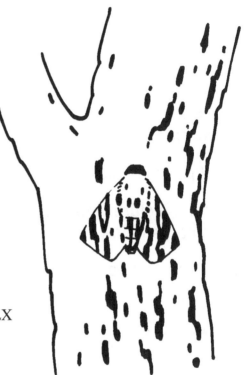

Content Area(s):

- life science

Objectives:

Students will . . .

- determine tactics animals use for camouflage.
- identify camouflaged animals.

Materials Required:

- computer with Internet access
- pencil or pen

Web Site(s):

- http://www.muohio.edu/dragonfly/hide/hidemap.HTMLX

Time:

approximately 25–35 minutes

Teaching the Lesson:

- With more advanced students, you can introduce the word "camouflage;" otherwise, refer to it as hiding or blending by using colors.
- This activity is for good readers or pairs of students.
- Go over the names of the animals that students locate in the drawing as a follow-up so they can compare each other's results.
- Make use of photographs, videos, or other media to give other examples of camouflage in nature.

SEEK, AND YOU MIGHT FIND IT *(cont.)*

Name:_____

Date:_____

Many animals are good at hiding themselves from other animals that want to eat them. They hide by using their colors, shapes, and sizes to match that of their surroundings.

Go to http://www.muohio.edu/dragonfly/hide/hidemap.HTMLX

Click on the picture wherever you think you see an animal hiding. Then write down its name below. If you are very careful, you might find all 22 animals.

Here are the names of the animals I found:

_____   _____

_____   _____

_____   _____

_____   _____

_____   _____

_____   _____

_____   _____

_____   _____

OLD BONES

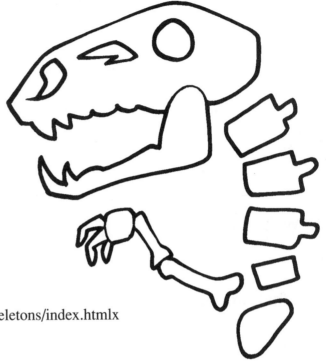

Content Area(s):

- life science
- earth science

Objectives:

Students will . . .

- investigate research completed by a scientist.
- record information about fossils.

Materials Required:

- computer with Internet access
- pencil or pen

Web Site(s):

- http://miavx1.acs.muohio.edu/~dragonfly/skeletons/index.htmlx

Time:

approximately 25–35 minutes

Teaching the Lesson:

- Bring in some fossils, if possible, for students to observe. Explain to them why fossils are of value to science.
- This activity is for advanced students or pairs of students.
- Discuss with the class the answers to the last question in the activity.
- Compare dinosaur fossils to fossils of other creatures.

OLD BONES *(cont.)*

Name:_____

Date:_____

Go to http://miavx1.acs.muohio.edu/~dragonfly/skeletons/index.htmlx and read about the person named Rudolfo who searches for dinosaur bones on this Web page. Then find the answers to the questions below.

1. What is the name of the country where Rudolfo searches for bones?

   _____

2. What does carnivorous mean? _____

   _____

3. What are fossils? _____

   _____

4. What do you call a scientist who studies fossils? _____

   _____

5. If you found a fossil bone of a dinosaur in your school playground, how do you think it might have gotten there?_____

   _____

   _____

   _____

   _____

HOWLING WOLVES

Content Area(s):

- life science

Objectives:

Students will . . .

- learn about wolf communication.
- practice communication skills as a "wolf."

Materials Required:

- computer with Internet access
- pencil or pen

Web Site(s):

- http://miavx1.acs.muohio.edu/~dragonfly/com/
- http://miavx1.acs.muohio.edu/~dragonfly/com/games.htmlx

Time:

approximately 25–35 minutes

Teaching the Lesson:

- Go over the topic of communication prior to this activity. Discuss how humans communicate and introduce the topic of animal communication (barking, singing, etc).
- This activity is for advanced students or pairs of students.
- Discuss with students the reasons for pack behavior among wolves and humans. Be sure they relate packs to family groups. You can also discuss nonverbal communication and play a sort of "charades" game to make the point of how nonverbal communication works.

HOWLING WOLVES *(cont.)*

Name:_____

Date:_____

Go to http://miavx1.acs.muohio.edu/~dragonfly/com/

What does a dog's bark mean? What are wolves trying to say when they howl in the night? Some scientists are trying to find out how wolves "talk" to one another, or communicate.

Read about wolves on this Web page. Then find the answers to the questions below.

1. What are two ways that wolves communicate? _____

_____

_____

_____

2. Why do you think wolves live together in groups or "packs"? _____

_____

_____

_____

Go to http://miavx1.acs.muohio.edu/~dragonfly/com/games.htmlx

Follow the directions and see if you can "talk" like a wolf!

COLORFUL CRAYONS

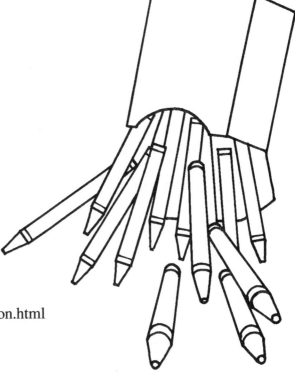

Content Area(s):

- physical science
- technology

Objectives:

Students will . . .

- explore a virtual crayon factory.
- determine how crayons are manufactured.

Materials Required:

- computer with Internet access
- pencil or pen

Web Site(s):

- http://www.crayola.com/assembly/how_crayon.html

Time:

approximately 25–35 minutes

Teaching the Lesson:

- Ask students, using several common classroom objects, how they believe these things are made. Focus on crayons and launch them into this activity.
- This activity is for good readers or pairs of students.
- Use this activity as a steppingstone to introduce students to the topic of manufacturing products they use, or "Where does it come from?"

COLORFUL CRAYONS *(cont.)*

Name:_____

Date:_____

You probably use crayons at school. Have you ever wondered how they are made? Let's visit the crayon factory to find out.

Go to http://www.crayola.com/assembly/how_crayon.html read about the crayons on this and the following Web pages. Answer the questions below.

1. What are the two main ingredients needed to make a crayon? _____

_____

_____

2. Where is the wax used for crayons stored?_____

_____

Click the "next" crayon at the bottom of the Web page.

3. What is pigment? _____

_____

Go to the "next" page.

4. What is happening in this picture?_____

_____

Go to the "next" page.

5. What is your favorite crayon color? Write the names of three things that are your favorite color. _____

_____

_____

EAT YOUR FRUITS AND VEGETABLES!

Content Area(s):

- life science

Objectives:

Students will . . .

- investigate facts about fruits and vegetables.
- record information about fruits and vegetables.

Materials Required:

- computer with Internet access
- pencil or pen

Web Site(s):

- http://www.dole5aday.com/cool/cool.html

Time:

approximately 25–35 minutes

Teaching the Lesson:

- Use this as part of a health/diet unit or as part of a plant unit.
- This activity is for good readers or pairs of students.
- Bring in some samples of fruits and vegetables so students can recite in front of the class facts that they have learned about these plants.

EAT YOUR FRUITS AND VEGETABLES! *(cont.)*

Name:_____

Date:_____

Go to http://www.dole5aday.com/cool/cool.html

On this Web page you will find out some neat things about different fruits and vegetables. Click on two different fruits or vegetables. Answer the questions about each one that you learn on this Web site.

1. Did you choose a fruit or vegetable? _____

_____

2. What is this fruit or vegetable called? _____

_____

3. Write down two interesting things you learned about your fruit or vegetable.

_____

_____

_____

Go back and click on another fruit or vegetable.

4. Did you choose a fruit or vegetable? _____

_____

5. What is this fruit or vegetable called? _____

_____

6. Write down two cool things you learned about your fruit or vegetable.

_____

_____

MAKE YOUR OWN DINOSAUR!

Content Area(s):

- life science

Objectives:

Students will . . .

- create virtual dinosaurs.
- draw their dinosaurs and write about them.

Materials Required:

- computer with Internet access
- pencil or pen
- drawing materials

Web Site(s):

- http://www.kidspace.com/kids/dinosaurs/createasaurus/

Time:

approximately 25–35 minutes

Teaching the Lesson:

- Discuss the fact that our knowledge of dinosaur skin color and some other characteristics is uncertain.
- This activity is for good readers or pairs of students.
- Share the drawings of the dinosaurs with the class.
- Go over a list of the different dinosaur types that students chose to create.

MAKE YOUR OWN DINOSAUR! *(cont.)*

Name:_____

Date:_____

Go to http://www.kidspace.com/kids/dinosaurs/createasaurus/

This Web page lets you make a dinosaur look just the way you want it to look. The first thing you need to do is click on the shape of the dinosaur. Its name will appear on the box. Write down the name of your dinosaur below.

1. My dinosaur is called a _____

Now pick out the color and shape of your dinosaur. Click on any box that you like.

2. What colors does your dinosaur have on it? _____

   _____

   _____

3. Do the same thing all over again but pick a different dinosaur. Write down its name and color._____

   _____

   _____

4. Draw a picture of your dinosaur below.

PUZZLING ANIMALS

Content Area(s):

- life science

Objectives:

Students will . . .

- unscramble animal puzzles.
- list unscrambled animal names.

Materials Required:

- computer with Internet access
- pencil or pen

Web Site(s):

- http://www.vpservices.com/vps/nwf/games/mix/mixgame.pl

Time:

approximately 25–35 minutes

Teaching the Lesson:

- Be sure that students can manipulate the puzzle pieces easily, or they will become frustrated.
- This activity is appropriate for less advanced students or pairs of students.
- You may choose to print out some of the successfully unscrambled puzzles.

PUZZLING ANIMALS *(cont.)*

Name:_____

Date:_____

Go to http://www.vpservices.com/vps/nwf/games/mix/mixgame.pl

Try to make an animal by changing the parts that don't match. Just click on the parts until you get a recognizable animal, and you win.

Play the game until you make at least four animals with the puzzle. Then draw the animals below.

HERD THOSE SHEEP

Content Area(s):

- life science

Objectives:

Students will . . .

- virtually "herd" a flock of sheep into a pen.
- record information about the uses of sheep in farming.

Materials Required:

- computer with Internet access
- pencil or pen

Web Site(s):

- http://www.mca.com/home/babe/game/

Time:

approximately 25–35 minutes

Teaching the Lesson:

- Use this activity as an introduction to farming or domestication of animals for human use.
- Be sure to note for students that the use of a pig to herd sheep is not normal practice among farmers.
- This activity is for average-level students or pairs of students.
- Follow up this activity by listing other domestic animals that are used as food or as tools (such as a dog).

HERD THOSE SHEEP *(cont.)*

Name:_____

Date:_____

In this game, you will help a pig to herd a flock of sheep into their pen.

Go to http://www.mca.com/home/babe/game/

Click on the space you think the pig needs to go to, to move the sheep toward their pen. Have fun. Then answer the questions below.

1. What is a group of sheep called? _____

   _____

2. What are two ways that sheep are used on farms? _____

   _____

3. What is a baby sheep called? _____

   _____

4. What animal does a farmer usually use to herd his flock of sheep?

   _____

   _____

BEING GREEN

Content Area(s):

- life science
- ecology

Objectives:

Students will . . .

- explore the meaning of "green" and recycling.
- determine how "green" their home and school are.

Materials Required:

- computer with Internet access
- pencil or pen

Web Site(s):

- http://www.teraplanning.com/cgi-bin/QuizGr.cgi

Time:

approximately 25–35 minutes

Teaching the Lesson:

- Make use of this activity as an introduction to recycling.
- Depending on when during a recycling unit you do this activity, students may do poorly on the quiz, so use it as a learning experience when looking at the correct answers.
- This activity is for good readers or pairs of students.
- You can expand the green survey to cover other places that students encounter in their lives.

BEING GREEN *(cont.)*

Name:_____

Date:_____

Today, being "green" doesn't mean that you came from another planet. It means that you care about our planet, Earth.

Go to http://www.teraplanning.com/cgi-bin/QuizGr.cgi

Take the "green" quiz to see if you and your family are doing all you can to keep our planet healthy.

1. What was your green rating after you answered all the questions? _____

   _____

2. Write down five things that you can do differently at home to be more "green." _____

   _____

   _____

   _____

   _____

3. Is your school green? Write down three things that you can do to help your class become more green. _____

   _____

   _____

   _____

   _____

JUST THE BEAR FACTS

Content Area(s):

- life science

Objectives:

Students will . . .

- research habits and characteristics of bears.
- record information learned about bears.

Materials Required:

- computer with Internet access
- pencil or pen

Web Site(s):

- http://www.nature-net.com/bears/cubden.html

Time:

approximately 25–35 minutes

Teaching the Lesson:

- If you wish to integrate literature into a science unit, this is an ideal topic since there are many popular stories written about bears
- This activity is for good readers or pairs of students.
- Have students do reports on a particular type of bear as an extension.
- You can also have students write a play about a bear or bear family and act it out in class.

JUST THE BEAR FACTS *(cont.)*

Name:_____

Date:_____

Go to http://www.nature-net.com/bears/cubden.html

At the bottom of the Web page are ten facts about bears. Read them and find the answers to the questions below.

1. Are bears small or large animals?_____

_____

2. Do bears have a good sense of smell?_____

_____

3. How do bears try to see and smell things better?_____

_____

_____

4. How many kinds of bears are there?_____

_____

5. What is the name of the smallest kind of bear? _____

_____

6. What do most bears eat? _____

_____

7. What kind of bear lives on the ice in the Arctic Ocean? _____

_____

OUR SOLAR SYSTEM

Content Area(s):

- earth science
- space science

Objectives:

Students will . . .

- read about the solar system and celestial bodies.
- record information about the above topics.

Materials Required:

- computer with Internet access
- pencil or pen

Web Site(s):

- http://heasarc.gsfc.nasa.gov/docs/StarChild/solar_system_level1/solar_system.html

Time:

approximately 25–35 minutes

Teaching the Lesson:

- Use this as a culminating activity for an earth/space science unit.
- This activity is for advanced students or pairs of students.
- Have students create drawings or posters of the solar system when they finish.
- Advanced students can be used as peer tutors for this subject matter to pair with less advanced pupils.

OUR SOLAR SYSTEM *(cont.)*

Name:_____

Date:_____

Go to http://heasarc.gsfc.nasa.gov/docs/StarChild/solar_system_level1/solar_system.html and read about our solar system and the planets on this Web page. Click on any links to find out what a word means. Then answer the questions below.

1. What is in our solar system? _____

_____

_____

2. What is in the center of the solar system? _____

_____

3. How many planets are in our solar system? _____

_____

4. What is a comet? _____

_____

_____

5. Name the nine planets. (**HINT:** Click on "The Planets" link.) _____

_____

_____

_____

_____

_____

SOLAR SYSTEM MATCHING

 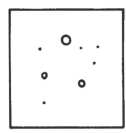 

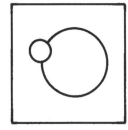 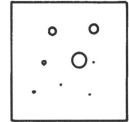

Content Area(s):

- earth science

Objectives:

Students will . . .

- match space images to each other in a concentration game.
- answer questions about the solar system.

Materials Required:

- computer with Internet access
- pencil or pen

Web Site(s):

- http://heasarc.gsfc.nasa.gov/docs/StarChild/solar_system_level1/match.html
- http://heasarc.gsfc.nasa.gov/docs/StarChild/solar_system_level1/solar_system_shuffle.html

Time:

approximately 25–35 minutes

Teaching the Lesson:

- Use this activity as enrichment or a culminating activity on the solar system and celestial bodies.
- This activity is for advanced students or pairs of students.
- Be sure that students keep their scores when playing the matching game so they get immediate feedback on their success over time.

SOLAR SYSTEM MATCHING! *(cont.)*

Name:_____

Date:_____

Go to
http://heasarc.gsfc.nasa.gov/docs/StarChild/solar_system_level1/match.html

Match the pictures of planets, asteroids, and the moon and stars by typing the number of the picture under its match.

1. What was your score after you finished?_____

_____

Go to http://heasarc.gsfc.nasa.gov/docs/StarChild/solar_system_level1/solar_system_shuffle.html

Try to match the cards with the questions about the solar system. Then check your answers!

2. What was your score? _____

_____

3. Which planet has over 1,000 rings? _____

_____

4. Where would you find the Great Red Spot? _____

_____

5. What is the hottest planet? _____

_____

INTO ORBITS WE GO

Content Area(s):

- earth science
- space science

Objectives:

Students will . . .

- determine the orbits of the planets in the solar system.
- match the correct orbit with each planet.

Materials Required:

- computer with Internet access
- pencil or pen

Web Site(s):

- http://heasarc.gsfc.nasa.gov/docs/StarChild/solar_system_level1/planet_go.html

Time:

approximately 25–35 minutes

Teaching the Lesson:

- Take time to explain the concept of orbits to the students before doing this activity. If they have memorized the order of the nine planets, this will be a review for them.
- This activity is for good readers or pairs of students.
- Some advanced thinkers may realize that the orbits of the planets cross one another. Tell them to answer the questions as the orbits are shown on the Web page.

INTO ORBITS WE GO *(cont.)*

Name:_____

Date:_____

Go to http://heasarc.gsfc.nasa.gov/docs/StarChild/solar_system_level1/planet_go.html

You have learned by now that the nine planets move around the sun in a pattern called an orbit. Your job in this activity is to find which planet belongs in each orbit in the picture on the Web page. Then write down the name of each planet in the correct orbit below.

Name of Planet

Orbit One: _____

Orbit Two: _____

Orbit Three: _____

Orbit Four: _____

Orbit Five: _____

Orbit Six: _____

Orbit Seven: _____

Orbit Eight: _____

Orbit Nine: _____

SPACE WORDS TO KNOW

Content Area(s):

- astronomy

Objectives:

Students will . . .

- identify space-related words.
- define at least two space-related words.

Materials Required:

- computer with Internet access
- pencil or pen

Web Site(s):

- http://heasarc.gsfc.nasa.gov/docs/StarChild/space_level1/world.html

Time:

approximately 25–35 minutes

Teaching the Lesson:

- You may wish to model for some students how to find one or two of the words in this puzzle.
- This activity is for good readers or pairs of students.
- Students can expand on the definitions as an extension activity.

SPACE WORDS TO KNOW *(cont.)*

Name:_____

Date:_____

Go to http://heasarc.gsfc.nasa.gov/docs/StarChild/space_level1/world.html

Try to find all the space words that are on the puzzle. The letters in each word light up when you find them.

Write each word that you find below.

1. _____

2. _____

3. _____

4. _____

5. _____

Bonus: Explain what two of the words on your list mean.

1. _____

_____

_____

2. _____

_____

_____

A TRIP TO THE ZOO

Content Area(s):

- life science

Objectives:

Students will . . .

- observe animals in a virtual zoo.
- compare traits of different animals and record results.

Materials Required:

- computer with Internet access
- pencil or pen

Web Site(s):

- http://library.advanced.org/11922/index.htm

Time:

approximately 25–35 minutes

Teaching the Lesson:

- Students should be prepared for careful observations during this activity so they can make reasonable conclusions.
- This activity is for individual students or pairs of students.
- You can expand this activity to include as much of the virtual zoo as you wish, time permitting.

A TRIP TO THE ZOO *(cont.)*

Name:_____

Date:_____

One of the best ways to learn about animals is to visit them at the zoo. Instead of getting on a bus and going to a real zoo, you are going to visit a "virtual" zoo.

Go to http://library.advanced.org/11922/index.htm

1. Let's begin at the reptile house. Click on it to see what's inside. At the bottom of the page is a list of the reptiles on display. Name them below.

   _____

   _____

   _____

2. Click on the turtle and then click on the snake. Write down how the turtle and snake are different. _____

   _____

   _____

   _____

3. Next we will visit Monkey Island. Click on the island and go to the bottom of the Web page. Here you will find monkeys and apes. Name one of each below. _____

   _____

4. How do monkeys and apes look different? _____

   _____

   _____

   _____

FINS, TAILS, AND MORE

Content Area(s):

• life science

Objectives:

Students will . . .

• identify external features of whales.

• record what they learn about each part of a whale.

Materials Required:

• computer with Internet access

• pencil or pen

Web Site(s):

• http://www.whaletimes.org/whapuz.htm

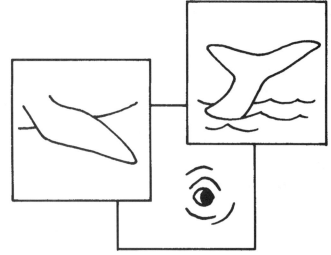

Time:

approximately 25–35 minutes

Teaching the Lesson:

• Use this activity as part of a marine mammal unit. Many of the concepts apply to animals other than whales.

• This activity is for good readers or pairs of students.

• Encourage students to write answers in complete sentences. They can compare answers with their neighbors and then fill in any gaps they have.

• You can have students make posters of what they learned as an extension.

FINS, TAILS, AND MORE *(cont.)*

Name:_____

Date:_____

Go to http://www.whaletimes.org/whapuz.htm

On this Web page activity you are going to find out what the different parts of a whale are. After you get the correct answers to questions, write down what you learned below.

Question One:
   What I learned . . . _____

_____

Question Two:
   What I learned . . . _____

_____

Question Three:
   What I learned . . . _____

_____

Question Four:
   What I learned . . . _____

_____

Question Five:
   What I learned . . . _____

_____

BE GOOD TO NATURE

Content Area(s):

- life science
- ecology

Objectives:

Students will . . .

- identify wasteful or polluting human activities in a drawing.
- record what is found in their observations.

Materials Required:

- computer with Internet access
- pencil or pen

Web Site(s):

- http://www.epa.gov/kids/whatswrong.htm

Time:

approximately 25–35 minutes

Teaching the Lesson:

- Students should have prior to this activity some basic idea of human practices that are wasteful of resources or cause pollution in the environment.
- This activity is for individuals or pairs of students.
- There are many possible extensions to this, including posters, plays, and modeling for parents. A display for parent-teacher night is a further extension toward community service by the students.

BE GOOD TO NATURE *(cont.)*

Name:_____

Date:_____

Go to http://www.epa.gov/kids/whatswrong.htm

On this page there is a picture for you to look at. Look carefully, and you will see that some of the people are doing things that can hurt our environment. Click everywhere you see things that are bad for our environment. Then write down what you clicked on below.

I clicked on _____

I clicked on _____

I clicked on _____

I clicked on _____

I clicked on _____

I clicked on _____

SAVE OUR CREATURES

Content Area(s):

- life science

Objectives:

Students will . . .

- identify endangered organisms.
- write down important information about each organism.

Materials Required:

- computer with Internet access
- pencil or pen

Web Site(s):

- http://www.epa.gov/kids/savespecies.htm

Time:

approximately 25–35 minutes

Teaching the Lesson:

- You may want to introduce the topic of extinction, endangered animals, and habitat destruction in this unit.
- This activity is for good readers or pairs of students.
- Brainstorm a list of animals that are already extinct as well as those that may soon become extinct after students are finished to check their understanding of the concepts presented here.

SAVE OUR CREATURES *(cont.)*

Name:_____

Date:_____

Go to http://www.epa.gov/kids/savespecies.htm

There are many reasons that animals, plants, and insects disappear forever. Most of the time it is because people are destroying their homes. On this Web page are pictures of creatures that are in danger of disappearing. Click on each one to find out more about it. Write down their names below.

My list of animals in danger of disappearing:

1. _____

2. _____

3. _____

4. _____

5. _____

6. _____

7. _____

8. _____

9. _____

10. _____

11. _____

12. _____

A WORLD FOR CHIPMUNKS

Content Area(s):

- life science

Objectives:

Students will . . .

- read a story about chipmunks in the wild.
- create their own part of the story.

Materials Required:

- computer with Internet access
- pencil or pen

Web Site(s):

- http://www.epa.gov/kids/chipmunk.htm

Time:

approximately 25–35 minutes

Teaching the Lesson:

- Before students continue with their own part of the story, spend time summarizing the story. In addition, try to have students use a tone similar to the original in their own writing.
- This activity is for good readers or pairs of students.
- You can vary this activity by having students expand on each other's stories as well and create a classroom book about chipmunks (or any other animals, for that matter).

A WORLD FOR CHIPMUNKS (cont.)

Name:_____

Date:_____

Go to http://www.epa.gov/kids/chipmunk.htm and read the story about the chipmunk on this and the following Web pages. Click "next" after you finish each page. When you are done, write another page of this story. What do you think happens next to the chipmunk?

_____

_____

_____

_____

_____

_____

_____

_____

_____

_____

_____

_____

_____

_____

_____

CLEAN THAT WATER!

Content Area(s):

- physical science
- ecology/recycling

Objectives:

Students will . . .

- research methods of water treatment.
- unscramble water treatment terms.

Materials Required:

- computer with Internet access
- pencil or pen

Web Site(s):

- http://www.epa.gov/kids/watertreatment.htm

Time:

approximately 25–35 minutes

Teaching the Lesson:

- Brainstorm with students about how water gets polluted and why it needs to be treated before being released into the environment.
- This activity is for advanced students or pairs of students.
- Students can take an inventory of what they do each day that pollutes water so they see the relationship between themselves and the topic.
- Some students may wish to create a model of the water treatment process as a project.

CLEAN THAT WATER! *(cont.)*

Name:_____

Date:_____

Dirty water from your sink, toilet, and laundry needs to be cleaned before it goes back to nature and becomes drinking water again. This is called water treatment.

Go to http://www.epa.gov/kids/watertreatment.htm

On this page you can follow some dirty water as it is treated or cleaned. Click on each part of the water treatment. Unscramble the words and write them down below.

Water Treatment Word List:

1. _____

2. _____

3. _____

4. _____

5. _____

6. _____

Write down two ways that water becomes dirty after people use it.

1. _____

   _____

   _____

   _____

2. _____

   _____

   _____

   _____

HELP SAVE A TREE!

Content Area(s):

- life science
- ecology

Objectives:

Students will . . .

- play a game that involves saving trees.
- express how people can help to save trees.
- describe the effects of a world without trees.

Materials Required:

- computer with Internet access
- pencil or pen

Web Site(s):

- http://www.randomhouse.com/seussville/games/lorax/

Time:

approximately 25–35 minutes

Teaching the Lesson:

- Use this as an essential part of an ecology/recycling unit.
- This activity is for individual students or pairs of students.
- Be sure to make students aware of the need in our society for trees as a resource to be used to build things as well as preserve.

HELP SAVE A TREE! *(cont.)*

Name:_____

Date:_____

Go to http://www.randomhouse.com/seussville/games/lorax/

Play the game to help save trees. Then write down four ways that people can save trees below.

Four Ways to Save Trees

1. _____

2. _____

3. _____

4. _____

Write a few sentences below about what the world will be like in the future if we do not try to save our trees today.

_____

_____

_____

_____

_____

_____

_____

_____

ARE YOU ALLERGIC?

Content Area(s):

- life science

Objectives:

Students will . . .

- determine the meaning of allergies.
- list different allergens.

Materials Required:

- computer with Internet access
- pencil or pen

Web Site(s):

- http://www.allergy-info.com/game.html

Time:

approximately 25–35 minutes

Teaching the Lesson:

- Preview the concepts presented in this unit with the students. Make sure they are aware that an allergen is something that causes a person's allergies to act up.
- This activity is for good readers or pairs of students.
- Generate a list of things that students in the class are allergic to. Have them explain their symptoms to the other students. This will personalize the topic for all pupils.

ARE YOU ALLERGIC? *(cont.)*

Name:_____

Date:_____

Many people get the sniffles, runny noses, or worse when they have allergies. Allergies only bother people when they are near something they are allergic to. If you are allergic to cats, they may make you sneeze. If you are allergic to strawberries, you may get bumps or a rash on your skin.

Go to http://www.allergy-info.com/game.html

Try to match the allergens on this web page. Then answer the questions below.

1. Does anyone in your family have allergies? _____

   _____

2. What are they allergic to? _____

   _____

3. Hay fever is one kind of allergy. What do you think hay fever is?_____

   _____

   _____

4. Let's say that you are allergic to cats. You sit on a chair and begin sneezing. There is no cat anywhere near you. Why do you think you are still sneezing? _____

   _____

   _____

   _____

ZIT BACK AND RELAX

Content Area(s):

- life science

Objectives:

Students will . . .

- explore the cause of pimples.
- record information about proper pimple treatment.
- virtually pop a pimple.

Materials Required:

- computer with Internet access
- pencil or pen

Web Site(s):

- http://www.osc.on.ca/JustFun/InteractiveZone/Zit/zit.htm

Time:

approximately 25–35 minutes

Teaching the Lesson:

- Even though students at this age level may not have acne, all of them are aware of the condition. They should be aware of the science and health issues behind this common problem.
- This activity is for good readers or pairs of students.
- Be prepared for lots of comments when students finally pop the zit. They will most likely want to do it several times. Remind them that they may not squeeze it until they finish answering the questions.

ZIT BACK AND RELAX *(cont.)*

Name:_____

Date:_____

Most people will have pimples some time in their lives. Do you know someone with pimples? They are perfectly normal, everyday things. What causes them? And what do they look like when they pop? Sound gross? Let's find out.

Go to http://www.osc.on.ca/JustFun/InteractiveZone/Zit/zit.htm

Before "squeezing" the zit, read about how zits happen at the bottom of the page. Answer the questions below.

1. Why shouldn't you squeeze a pimple? _____

_____

_____

2. What kinds of glands get clogged when a pimple appears?_____

_____

_____

3. What is another word for white blood cells that die? _____

_____

_____

Okay, if you really want to, you may now "squeeze" the zit at the top of this page.

4. What happened? _____

_____

_____

_____

FROGGY TIME!

Content Area(s):

- life science

Objectives:

Students will . . .

- construct a frog puzzle.
- match frog pictures and colors.

Materials Required:

- computer with Internet access
- pencil or pen

Web Site(s):

- http://www.big.or.jp/~frog/game/zigsaw.html
- http://www.big.or.jp/~frog/game/color.html

Time:

approximately 25–35 minutes

Teaching the Lesson:

- Use this as part of an amphibian unit to reinforce concepts of frogs' feeding habits.
- This activity is for individuals or pairs of students.
- The second puzzle/matching game is a challenge, so provide adequate time for students to give it a good try.

FROGGY TIME! *(cont.)*

Name:_____

Date:_____

Frogs are some of the most interesting of all animals. They are colorful, great jumpers, and, best of all, they love to eat flies. Let's see if you can put together a puzzle of a frog waiting for its next meal.

Go to http://www.big.or.jp/~frog/game/zigsaw.html

Click and hold on each piece of the puzzle as you put the pieces together. Have fun.

After you have finished the puzzle, write down three sentences about what you think the frog might be thinking while it waits for a fly to come close.

_____

_____

_____

_____

_____

_____

_____

_____

Go to http://www.big.or.jp/~frog/game/color.html

Play the frog game. Try to match the frog pictures and colors. It's not easy, but it is fun.

YOU ARE EATING RIGHT, RIGHT?

Content Area(s):

- life science
- health

Objectives:

Students will . . .

- create a virtual daily menu.
- assess the nutritional value of their choices online.

Materials Required:

- computer with Internet access
- pencil or pen

Web Site(s):

- http://www.bennygoodsport.com/food.htm

Time:

approximately 25–35 minutes

Teaching the Lesson:

- This could be a culminating activity or an introductory activity for a unit on food and diet.
- This activity is for good readers or pairs of students.
- Some background information about what constitutes a good diet would help students to make this more meaningful.
- As an extension, have students assess the food provided by the school cafeteria.

YOU ARE EATING RIGHT, RIGHT? *(cont.)*

Name:_____

Date:_____

Go to http://www.bennygoodsport.com/food.htm

Here you will find a list of foods to choose from. Your job is to pick out the most healthful food for every meal of the day. Click on the box next to each food. Write down below your list for each meal. When you finish, click "How Healthful Am I?"

Healthful Breakfast Foods:

_____

_____

Healthful Lunch Foods:

_____

_____

Healthful Snacks:

_____

_____

Healthful Dinner Foods:

_____

_____

Now Click "How Healthful Am I?" Did you choose the most healthful foods?

_____

_____

EAT OR BE EATEN

Content Area(s):

- life science

Objectives:

Students will . . .

- explore ocean food webs.
- answer questions about food webs involving fish.
- avoid being eaten in a fish game.

Materials Required:

- computer with Internet access
- pencil or pen

Web Site(s):

- http://www.gamescene.com/somethingfishy.html

Time:

approximately 25–35 minutes

Teaching the Lesson:

- Students should understand the basic ideas behind predator/prey relationships, including those that involve humans using animals for food.
- This activity is for good readers or pairs of students.
- As an extension, have students construct a food web diagram of the predators and prey seen in the game they play online.

EAT OR BE EATEN *(cont.)*

Name:_____

Date:_____

In nature, animals must eat other things to live. Sometimes an animal will get eaten by another if it isn't careful. Here is your chance to try life as a fish.

Go to http://www.gamescene.com/somethingfishy.html

Your small yellow fish must eat to live. You need to make sure that it eats small fish. At the same time, bigger fish are trying to eat your fish. Play the game— and don't get eaten.

1. What are two ways that a small fish in the ocean can keep from being eaten? _____

   _____

   _____

   _____

2. Think of three animals that eat other animals. Write them down below.

   _____

   _____

3. Think of three animals that might get eaten by other animals. Write them down below. _____

   _____

4. Many people eat animals. Write down three kinds of animals that people eat. _____

   _____

   _____

BUILD A CUSTOM CAR

Content Area(s):

- technology
- physical science

Objectives:

Students will . . .

- create a virtual car.
- write a story about driving the car.

Materials Required:

- computer with Internet access
- pencil or pen

Web Site(s):

- http://freezone.com/fun_games/ultwheels

Time:

approximately 25–35 minutes

Teaching the Lesson:

- Have a discussion with students about cars, airplanes, and other transportation vehicles prior to this activity.
- This activity is for individuals or pairs of students.
- Challenged readers/writers could draw a set of cartoons depicting themselves driving the car and give an oral report instead of writing the story.
- Show students pictures of the various types of cars, such as off-road, drag racers, etc., so they set goals when constructing their cars.

BUILD A CUSTOM CAR *(cont.)*

Name:_____

Date:_____

Go to http://freezone.com/fun_games/ultwheels

You finally have a chance to make that cool car you have always wanted. It might be a drag racer, off-road machine, or super street rod. Click on all the cool parts you want and see what it looks like.

Draw a picture of your car below. Write a short story about what it is like to drive your car.

_____

_____

_____

_____

_____

_____

WHERE DID IT GO?

Content Area(s):

- life science

Objectives:

Students will . . .

- locate camouflaged animals in a picture.
- analyze camouflage and coloration warning tactics among animals.

Materials Required:

- computer with Internet access
- pencil or pen

Web Site(s):

- http://www.exploratorium.edu/exhibits/disappearing_act/shock_dis_act.html

Time:

approximately 25–35 minutes

Teaching the Lesson:

- Discuss with students the reasons animals have bright or camouflaged bodies. Explain that bright colors provide warning to predators while camouflaged animals tend to hide from predators.
- This activity is for good readers or pairs of students.
- Have students create posters of different animals with these color patterns as an extension.
- You can have advanced students find pictures of animals and determine what the reasons for their color patterns are.

WHERE DID IT GO? *(cont.)*

Name:_____

Date:_____

Do you know of any animals that can blend into their surroundings? Fish, birds, beetles—many kinds of animals blend in to keep from being eaten. They also do it so they can hide and catch another animal as food.

Go to

http://www.exploratorium.edu/exhibits/disappearing_act/shock_dis_act.html

Look at the picture and try to find what is hidden there. Then follow the directions so you can see it.

1. Small animals often hide by blending into their environments. Name three animals that you think might do this. _____

   _____

   _____

2. Some animals are brightly colored because they want to be seen. Why? Because they may be poisonous to eat. Other animals learn not to eat brightly colored bugs and frogs. Write down three brightly colored animals below. _____

   _____

   _____

GOING BATTY!

Content Area(s):

- life science

Objectives:

Students will . . .

- examine some of the myths and truths about bats.
- answer questions relating to bats.

Materials Required:

- computer with Internet access
- pencil or pen

Web Site(s):

- http://members.aol.com/bats4kids/

Time:

approximately 25–35 minutes

Teaching the Lesson:

- Discuss bat myths with the students prior to this activity.
- This activity is for good readers or pairs of students.
- Advanced students can write a story about a fruit bat that everyone is afraid of because of rumors and myths that prove untrue.
- In some classrooms, building a bat box is an excellent extension activity that will allow students to study the animals up close and help them survive.

GOING BATTY! *(cont.)*

Name:_____

Date:_____

Are you afraid of bats? Many people think bats are scary creatures. Most bats are not harmful to people. Let's find out more.

Go to http://members.aol.com/bats4kids/

Answer the following questions.

1. Write down four things that are not true about bats. _____

_____

_____

_____

2. Where do most bats live? _____

_____

3. What do bats eat? _____

_____

_____

4. How can bats help people? _____

_____

_____

_____

_____

IT'S A RAT GAME

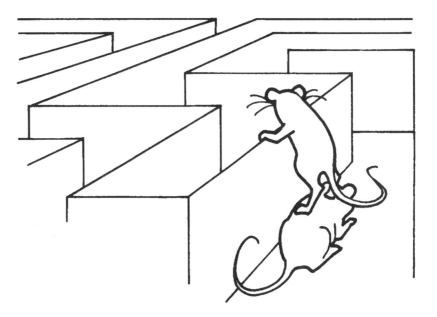

Content Area(s):

- life science

Objectives:

Students will . . .

- race a virtual rat through a maze.
- record the results of several races.

Materials Required:

- computer with Internet access
- pencil or pen

Web Site(s):

- http://www.amused.com/games/ratrace.html

Time:

approximately 25–35 minutes

Teaching the Lesson:

- Spend time explaining to students the variables they can change in this game. Be sure to play it yourself before beginning. They should be made aware of what intelligence means and how it affects rat performance in the maze.

- This activity is for advanced students or pairs of students.

- You can help students come up with the "ideal" rat settings for speed and intelligence if the class keeps accurate records of the setting in each game as students race through the maze.

IT'S A RAT GAME *(cont.)*

Name:_____

Date:_____

Go to http://www.amused.com/games/ratrace.html

In this game you will "race" a rat through a maze. You have to play the game and change how smart he is and his speed.

Try to run a race through the maze. Write down all the settings for intelligence (smartness), speed, and other changes you make. Repeat the race three times. Then write down what the best combination of speed and intelligence is for rats.

Race One:_____

_____

_____

Race Two: _____

_____

_____

Race Three: _____

_____

_____

SPACE SCIENCE MATCHING

Content Area(s):

- astronomy

Objectives:

Students will . . .

- match different space images in a game.
- record information about space-related objects studied.

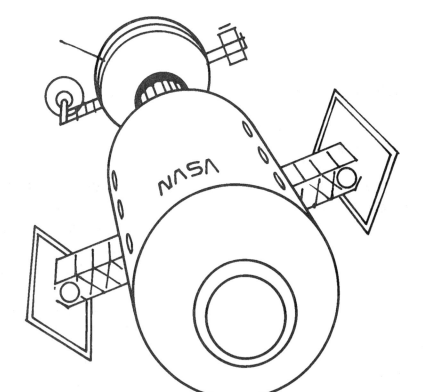

Materials Required:

- computer with Internet access
- pencil or pen

Web Site(s):

- http://www.seasky.org/sky4e.html

Time:

approximately 25–35 minutes

Teaching the Lesson:

- Some students will need assistance identifying what the objects are that they are matching.
- This activity is for individuals or pairs of students.
- Use this as part of an overall space science unit in which students are familiarized with at least some of the objects in the game.

SPACE SCIENCE MATCHING *(cont.)*

Name:_____

Date:_____

Go to http://www.seasky.org/sky4e.html

Play the matching game. See if you can match all the different space science pictures.

When you finish, write down the names of six things that you have matched in the game.

1. _____

2. _____

3. _____

4. _____

5. _____

6. _____

YOUR OWN COMPUTER FISH TANK!

Content Area(s):

- life science

Objectives:

Students will . . .

- create a virtual aquarium.
- record and interpret data about their aquarium.

Materials Required:

- computer with Internet access
- pencil or pen

Web Site(s):

- http://www.cfkc.demon.co.uk/javaquarium/aquarium.htm

Time:

approximately 25–35 minutes

Teaching the Lesson:

- If you have a classroom fish tank, students may be able to relate to this activity more readily.
- This activity is for good readers or pairs of students.
- Since this is a virtual ocean tank, students will need to know the types of animals they are dealing with in the fish tank. Be sure to provide them with some information about what they will encounter.
- The most important part of the learning experience in this activity is to find out what effect the changes students make have on the activity and health of creatures inside the tank. Be sure they keep accurate records so they can interpret the data.

YOUR OWN COMPUTER FISH TANK! *(cont.)*

Name:_____

Date:_____

Go to http://www.cfkc.demon.co.uk/javaquarium/aquarium.htm

You can make your computerized aquarium look any way you wish. You choose the number of fish, kinds of fish, and coral—it's up to you. Make your choices and then look at your aquarium. Then answer the questions below.

1. What background did you choose for your aquarium? _____

_____

2. What kind of fish did you choose for your aquarium? _____

_____

3. How many fish did you choose to put in your aquarium? _____

_____

4. Pretend you are talking to a friend on the telephone about your aquarium. Explain what it looks like so your friend can imagine what it looks like.

_____

_____

Now let's make another aquarium. This time choose a different number of fish, type of fish, and background.

5. How was this aquarium different from the first one? _____

_____

6. Which aquarium do you like better? Why? _____

_____

HIGH ENERGY FUN!

Content Area(s):

- physical science

Objectives:

Students will . . .

- research the energy sources on earth.
- decode a puzzle relating to energy.

Materials Required:

- computer with Internet access
- pencil or pen

Web Site(s):

- http://www.energy.ca.gov/education/puzzles/puzzles-html/sun0.html
- http://www.energy.ca.gov/education/puzzles/puzzles-html/crypto1.html

Time:

approximately 25–35 minutes

Teaching the Lesson:

- Prepare students for this activity with a discussion and lessons about energy use and its ultimate source, the sun.
- This activity is for advanced students or pairs of students.
- Unscrambling the code will be a challenge to all students. Pair them together for the greatest chance of success.

HIGH ENERGY FUN! *(cont.)*

Name:_____

Date:_____

Energy heats our homes and moves our cars. Energy runs our televisions and computer games. Without enough energy, life would be very different. Let's become energy experts.

Go to http://www.energy.ca.gov/education/puzzles/puzzles-html/sun0.html

Connect the dots to find out about our most important energy source.

What did you learn about energy in this puzzle? _____

_____

_____

Now see if you can find out the secret code words.

Go to http://www.energy.ca.gov/education/puzzles/puzzles-html/crypto1.html

Look carefully at the code word in the example. Write down what each letter means in the new code:

H means _____

O means _____

X means _____

K means _____

W means _____

Now try to crack the code. (**Hint:** Find only the letters that you know first.) You may work with a partner because this can be a challenge.

TAKING CARE OF TIGER

Content Area(s):

- life science

Objectives:

Students will . . .

- take care of a virtual tiger as a virtual zookeeper.
- observe effects of changes in the virtual tiger's diet and conditions.

Materials Required:

- computer with Internet access
- pencil or pen

Web Site(s):

- http://207.24.89.70/features/97/tigers

Time:

approximately 25–35 minutes

Teaching the Lesson:

- Students should be made aware of the threats to tigers in their natural environments and why they are kept in captivity.
- This activity is for good readers or pairs of students.
- Those students with pets at home (or if you have a classroom pet) will be familiar with the concepts presented here already.

TAKING CARE OF TIGER *(cont.)*

Name:_____

Date:_____

Go to http://207.24.89.70/features/97/tigers

Work as a team and try to take care of the rare tiger. You are the zookeeper so do a great job and keep the tiger happy.

Follow the directions on the Web page carefully. Answer the questions below.

1. What kind of "furniture" did you put in your tiger's home?_____

   _____

   _____

2. What did you choose to feed the tiger?_____

   _____

   _____

3. What toys did you pick for your tiger to play with? _____

   _____

   _____

4. Do you think taking care of a tiger is easy or hard? Why?_____

   _____

   _____

   _____

   _____

CAN YOU GUESS THE ANIMALS?

Content Area(s):

- life science

Objectives:

Students will . . .

- guess the identites of animals based on clues presented.
- record the animals they identify.

Materials Required:

- computer with Internet access
- pencil or pen

Web Site(s):

- http://www.zoobooks.com/canyouguess0.htm

Time:

approximately 25–35 minutes

Teaching the Lesson:

- You can make use of this general activity any time you wish to discuss animals with the students.
- This activity is for individual students or pairs of students.
- As an extension, have students write a brief report on several of the animals that they identify. They can use Internet resources to find out additional information about each one.

CAN YOU GUESS THE ANIMALS? *(cont.)*

Name:_____

Date:_____

Go to http://www.zoobooks.com/canyouguess0.htm

Here is your chance to show just how much you know about animals. Click on any target board to begin. List below the animals that you guess.

1. _____

2. _____

3. _____

4. _____

5. _____

6. _____

7. _____

8. _____

9. _____

10. _____

A DESERT VISIT

Content Area(s):

- life science

Objectives:

Students will . . .

- explore a virtual desert.
- record information about the desert biome.

Materials Required:

- computer with Internet access
- pencil or pen

Web Site(s):

- http://www.mobot.org/MBGnet/set1/desert/whatis.htm

Time:

approximately 25–35 minutes

Teaching the Lesson:

- When you are studying different biomes and/or habitats, use this activity as an introduction to the desert biome. You can dispel some of the myths about deserts as well, including many students' impressions that deserts are lifeless.
- This activity is for good readers or pairs of students.
- Examine several different deserts as a follow-up activity. Visit the Sahara, Mojave, and other deserts to compare the organisms that live there.

A DESERT VISIT *(cont.)*

Name:_____

Date:_____

Deserts are places that people think about when the weather is hot. When people think of deserts, they think of sand, dry winds, and cactus.

1. When you think of a desert, what do you think of? Use three words that show how you think of deserts. _____

   _____

Go to http://www.mobot.org/MBGnet/set1/desert/whatis.htm

Read about deserts. Find the answers to the questions below.

2. Are deserts always hot? _____

   _____

3. Why are deserts usually very dry? _____

   _____

4. What happens after the rain comes in a desert? _____

   _____

   _____

PENGUIN SCRAMBLE

Content Area(s):

- life science

Objectives:

Students will . . .

- unscramble penquin-related words online.
- write a short story about penguins.

Materials Required:

- computer with Internet access
- pencil or pen

Web Site(s):

- http://www.owl.on.ca/chick/puzfun.html

Time:

approximately 25–35 minutes

Teaching the Lesson:

- Discuss penguins and the arctic environment along with this activity. Compare them with other birds—both similarities and differences.
- This activity is for good readers or pairs of students.
- Some students may need help writing the story. As an alternative, have them use each word in a sentence.
- Make use of the virtual zoos online to find out more about penguins.

PENGUIN SCRAMBLE *(cont.)*

Name:_____

Date:_____

Go to http://www.owl.on.ca/chick/puzfun.html

Look at the pictures of the penguins. Try to change the scrambled words into real words. Write down the unscrambled words below.

1. _____

2. _____

3. _____

4. _____

5. Use all four words in a short story below about a penguin living on the ice at the North Pole.

_____

_____

_____

_____

_____

_____

_____

_____

_____

_____

SHIPWRECKED!

Content Area(s):

- physical science
- life science

Objectives:

Students will . . .

- attempt to escape from a virtual shipwreck.
- record all data they use to help them escape.

Materials Required:

- computer with Internet access
- pencil or pen

Web Site(s):

- http://www.muohio.edu/dragonfly/sounds/ship/index.htmlx

Time:

approximately 35–55 minutes

Teaching the Lesson:

- Prepare students for this challenging activity by previewing it. Pay particular attention to the lack of materials on the island and how they should make use of what they have available.
- This activity is for teams of advanced students in groups of three.
- Compare the progress of each team periodically throughout the period. Go around the room and provide advice if anyone gets stuck.

SHIPWRECKED! *(cont.)*

Name:_____

Date:_____

Go to http://www.muohio.edu/dragonfly/sounds/ship/index.htmlx

You are sailing along in the ocean and your boat sinks. You and two other people make it to a deserted island. On this Web site you and your team will try to find out everything you can to help you escape from the island.

As you complete the activity, write down what you have done or learned before you click to the next screen. Use as much space as you wish. Remember to write down everything before moving to the next screen.

1. _____

2. _____

3. _____

4. _____

5. _____

6. _____

7. _____

8. _____

9. _____

10. _____

11. _____

12. _____

13. _____

14. _____

15. _____

IT'S ABOUT TREES

Content Area(s):

- life science

Objectives:

Students will . . .

- examine different tree shapes.
- determine the advantage of each shape for a tree.
- draw a tree based on what they learn.

Materials Required:

- computer with Internet access
- pencil or pen
- drawing materials

Web Site(s):

- http://miavx1.muohio.edu/~dragonfly/trees.HTMLX

Time:

approximately 25–35 minutes

Teaching the Lesson:

- This activity is self-explanatory for good readers. A discussion will help lower-level students to understand the concept of tree shape and survival under different conditions.
- This activity is for good readers or pairs of students.
- Some students may need help picking out facts from those presented on the Web page to write down. You may wish to help some of them get started on this process.

ITS ABOUT TREES *(cont.)*

Name:_____

Date:_____

Go to http://miavx1.muohio.edu/~dragonfly/trees.HTMLX

Click on "the shapes of trees."

On this Web page, you will find lots of information about why trees are shaped in certain ways. Write down below five things you learn about trees.

Here are five things I learned about trees:

1. I learned that _____

   _____

2. I learned that _____

   _____

3. I learned that _____

   _____

4. I learned that _____

   _____

5. I learned that _____

   _____

6. Draw a picture of your favorite tree below. Write down why it has that shape.

MAKING TRACKS

Content Area(s):

- life science

Objectives:

Students will . . .

- match animal tracks to different animals.
- draw four sets of animal tracks.

Materials Required:

- computer with Internet access
- pencil or pen
- drawing materials

Web Site(s):

- http://www.vpservices.com/vps/nwf/games/match/matchgam.cgi

Time:

approximately 25–35 minutes

Teaching the Lesson:

- After students finish the activity, analyze the different footprints to see how the animals' feet are adapted for the environment in which they live.
- This activity is for individuals or pairs of students.
- Have students create additional puzzles for each other, using different animal tracks than those presented here.
- If possible, visit a creek or pond where real animal tracks can be found and identified.

MAKING TRACKS *(cont.)*

Name:_____

Date:_____

Go to http://www.vpservices.com/vps/nwf/games/match/matchgam.cgi

Tracks are animal footprints. Here you will try to find out what kind of animal the tracks are from. Click on the tracks to make your guess. Then draw a picture of the tracks made by each animal on the Web page.

1. Here are pig tracks:

2. Here are wood frog tracks:

3. Here are river otter tracks:

4. Here are mallard duck tracks: